A Keepsake

MAINE

Antelo Devereux Jr.

4880 Lower Valley Road • Atglen, PA 19310

Grindle Point Lighthouse, Islesboro

INTRODUCTION
Maine—the Way Life Should Be

The Red Paint People and, later, the Wabanaki—or people of the dawn—were the first human inhabitants of the territory they called Wabanakigok. European contact with the coast was possibly by Norsemen and certainly by John Cabot in the late 1400s. A settlement headed by George Popham was attempted in 1607. It failed, and the settlers who remained sailed back to England in the first boat built in Maine, a pinnace named *Virginia* (a replica was launched in Bath in 2022). As the New World was colonized, Maine was fought over by the French, Native Americans, and English. The latter eventually took control of the land as part of Massachusetts until it become the country's twenty-third state in 1820.

Maine flourished throughout most of the nineteenth century. Lumber, ice, granite, lime, and textiles, not to mention fishing, propelled its economy. Mills were constructed along the Kennebec, Penobscot, Androscoggin, and other rivers. Ships were built along the coast in such seaports as Belfast, Rockland, Damariscotta, and Bath. Towns both inland and along the coast grew. Large houses remain today as evidence of the great wealth of the times, as do mills and dams along the major rivers. Shipping also was a major industry, and many captains' and owners' houses still remain. Both standard- and narrow-gauge railroads were laid down to penetrate the vast areas inland and gain access to natural resources. To the very north, Aroostook County became known for its agriculture, most notably for potato farms.

As the US expanded and the center of economic gravity moved south and west, Maine's economy slowly declined. Today, paper and lumber mills are quiet and shipping is barely evident, but the remains of former activities are visible. Now tourism, hunting, fishing, and snowmobiling have taken over, both along the coasts and in various spots inland. More recently, Maine has seen a surge of people seeking permanent homes.

These ninety images capture bits of what remains from the old days and what makes the state a wonderful place to visit, travel, and live in today. They illustrate why Maine is "the way life should be."

Penobscot Bay

Islesboro

Belfast

Belfast

Kennebunk

Freedom

East Penobscot Bay

Pinnace Virginia, *Bath*

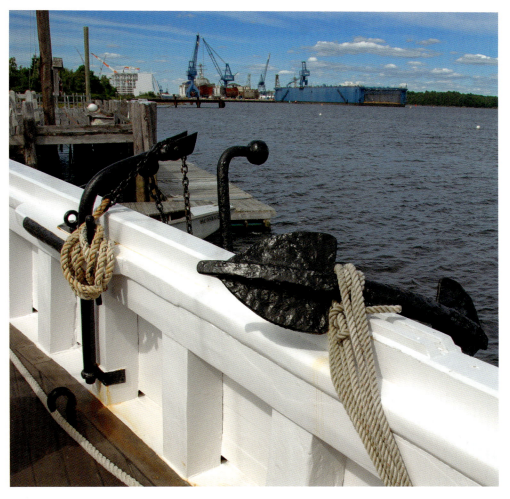

Bath

South Freeport

Shaker Village, Sabbathday Lake

Union

Freeport

New Portland

Rumford

Rumford

Rangeley

Bangor

Farmington

Moosehead Lake, Greenville

Moosehead Lake, Greenville

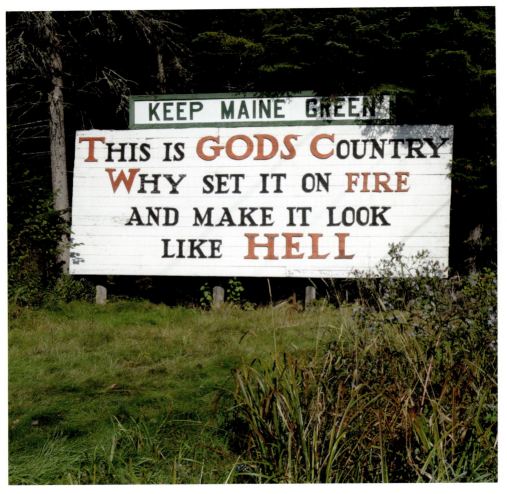

Moosehead Lake, Greenville

Kokadjo

Knox Mansion, Thomaston

Dover-Foxcroft

Alpacas, Common Ground Fair, Unity

Common Ground Fair, Unity

Fair, Camden

Kayaks

Blueberry field

Winter Harbor

Mount Katahdin, Millinocket

Moose

Deer

Trenton

Pemaquid Point

Camden

Ice fishing

Wild turkeys, Alna

Ice fishing, Kennebec River, Randolph

Fort Kent

Madawaska

Frenchville

Frenchville

Van Buren

Presque Isle

Prospect Harbor

Islesboro

Islesboro

Camden

Bug Lighthouse, Portland

Autumn blueberries

Waldoboro

Islesboro

Grindle Point, Islesboro

Eider duck

Beaver

Seal

Olson House, Cushing

Langlais Sculpture Preserve, Cushing

Colby College Museum of Art, Waterville

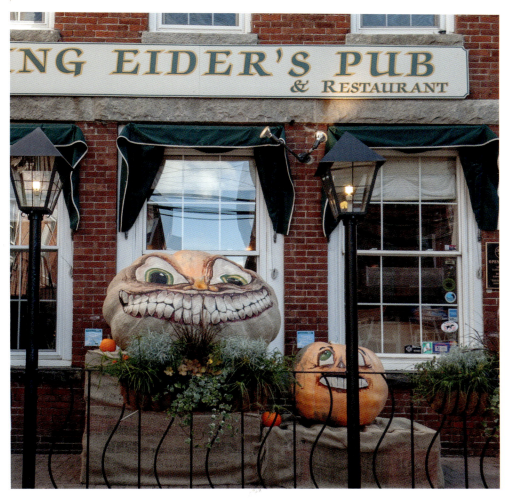

Damariscotta

Common Ground Fair, Unity

Rockland

Portland

Lobster fishing

Wiscasset

Nervous Nellie's Jams & Jellies, Deer Isle

Old-time music jam

Lawn mower racing

Birch trees

Jackman

Rangeley

Southwest Harbor

Wiscasset, Waterville & Farmington Railway, Alna

Seashore Trolley Museum, Kennebunkport

Lady Pepperrell House, Kittery

Coastal Maine Botanical Gardens, Boothbay

The Lost Kitchen, Freedom

Freedom

Dover-Foxcroft

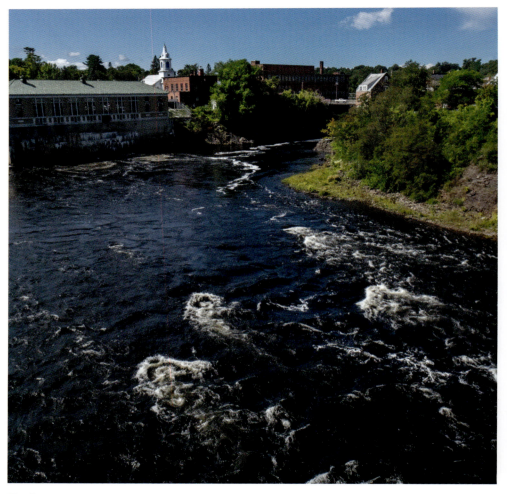

Skowhegan

Penobscot Bay

Portland

Portland

DeLorme/Garmin, Yarmouth

Bloodworm digging

Mount Desert

Penobscot Bay

Antelo Devereux Jr. has been photographing for the better part of his life, first as an amateur and more recently as a professional. He has published eleven travel-oriented books and has exhibited his images in various venues and galleries in Maine, Vermont, Pennsylvania, and Delaware. He has degrees from Harvard University and the University of Pennsylvania and has studied at Maine Media Workshops. He lives with his family in Chester County, Pennsylvania, and spends summers in Maine. His photographs can be seen on Instagram @photoeye1.

OTHER **SCHIFFER** **BOOKS** BY THE AUTHOR:

Coastal Maine: A Keepsake, 978-0-7643-5575-2

Maine: Out & About, 978-0-7643-3492-4

OTHER **SCHIFFER** **BOOKS** ON RELATED SUBJECTS:

Embracing Light: A Year in Acadia National Park & Mount Desert Island, Scott Erskine, 978-0-7643-5750-3

Sketchbook Traveler: New England, James Lancel McElhinney, 978-0-7643-6616-1

Copyright © 2024 by Antelo Devereux Jr.
Library of Congress Control Number: 2023941111

All rights reserved. No part of this work may be reproduced or used in any form or by any means—graphic, electronic, or mechanical, including photocopying or information storage and retrieval systems—without written permission from the publisher.

The scanning, uploading, and distribution of this book or any part thereof via the Internet or any other means without the permission of the publisher is illegal and punishable by law. Please purchase only authorized editions and do not participate in or encourage the electronic piracy of copyrighted materials.

"Schiffer," "Schiffer Publishing, Ltd.," and the pen and inkwell logo are registered trademarks of Schiffer Publishing, Ltd.

Designed by Danielle D. Farmer
Cover design by Jack Chappell
Type set in Bell MT/Bodoni URW

ISBN: 978-0-7643-6742-7
Printed in China

Published by Schiffer Publishing, Ltd.
4880 Lower Valley Road
Atglen, PA 19310
Phone: (610) 593-1777; Fax: (610) 593-2002
Email: info@schifferbooks.com
Web: www.schifferbooks.com

For our complete selection of fine books on this and related subjects, please visit our website at www.schifferbooks.com. You may also write for a free catalog.

Schiffer Publishing's titles are available at special discounts for bulk purchases for sales promotions or premiums. Special editions, including personalized covers, corporate imprints, and excerpts, can be created in large quantities for special needs. For more information, contact the publisher.